FROM HOOD

TO

HARVEST

Arry J. McNeill

FROM HOOD TO HARVEST

ISBN: 9781081767174

Divinely Inspired Publishers, Fayetteville NC

Cover Design: Chantee Cheek

Reflections

I was emotional writing this book because when I started writing this book, it took my mind back through what God has done in my life, the gratefulness in my heart towards you Lord, is unimaginable. Lord, you are my everything, and my life, my existence, my being, my Abba Father, faithful God, my healer and keeper, I can go on and on about you.

Thank you for blessing me with the chance to write this book. Now I understand why God had me journaling all those random writings years ago. I want to thank you for all you have done for me and my babies from then until now. I am so honored to have been called to do your will. I love you Lord.

I have learned that I am a Warrior in God, I will continue to persevere through life in God to fulfill and complete His plan for my life. Lord, I thank you for seeing the best in me, pass the unworthiness I presented to you, your love that you speak of in your Holy Word. It is the truth and you are so amazing, thank you from delivering me out of Egypt, and bringing me into a land of milk & honey.

Lord I just can't praise you or thank you enough, but I will do my best in showing you I truly love you, by living a Holy lifestyle, continue denying myself and my will and continually yield myself to your will, and become even more obedient to your Word.

Dedications and Special Thanks

In the Memory of my Parents Donnie Manning, Altory Manning, Helen Manning

To My Beloved Antonio "Biggie" Styles- I miss you so much baby, you have inspired and taught me so much in so many ways, while you were living and in your passing. You gave me the courage to finish this book. You were always a special child since birth, I had plans for us, but God's plan overpowered ours. You are now at peace and watching over us. I will continue to make sure your memory lives on through the ministry God birthed from. Mommy loves you Son #LLT

To My Children- Dequilla, I'rielle, Roderick— Mommy Loves you so much and I thank God for you, and for being my children, as much as I taught you, you taught me as well. All four of you changed my life in so many ways. We have been through the good, the bad, and worst of it, and God has carried us. God didn't just make Tone the only one born "Trained to Go" we were to.

To my Spiritual Dad, Spiritual Mothers, My God-moms, My God-Dad—Apostle Juan & Rosa Buatista Ronnie & Majorie McNeill, Mother L. Haire I love you all dearly, thank you for being in my life and for your love and patience, and most of all your prayers for me and my family. You all played a part in my life from my childhood all the way to my Adulthood. I know dealing with me and my children wasn't always easy, but when God gave you the job, none of you aborted the mission. You all stayed by our side and never judged; the loyalty is unforgettable. You all were there at my lowest points in my life to my best, and the in between. Sorry for the grey hairs. God gave you a special anointing to deal with me, Lord I thank you because it worked, you are seeing the Lord's handy work.

To my Three Best friends—Tiffany M. Sharon G. Polly S. There are no words to explain the loyalty from you Queens, our friendships have had some ups and downs, but you never left me hanging. From all the fun, good laughs, the tears we shed together, from some disagreements, etc. You guys Rock!! And just you know I'm not sharing you guys. You encouraged me and pushed me to my best went sometimes I felt like giving up, your prayers and love didn't go unseen or unheard. I truly thank God for putting you in my life. Thank you being standing with me while God was doing his work in my Life. You all got to see most of the beginning until now, and we all know he is not finished with me yet. I Love you!

To My Two Sisters—Rubeye Manning & Victoria Henry I Love you both dearly. Thank you for everything!!

To My Husband and Pastor—Elder William McNeill Thank You for helping with the process that The Lord has been doing in my life, thank you for the teachings, Revelation from the Lord, wisdom and knowledge of the Word of God that God releases through you.

Introduction

My Name is Arry Jay, an old soul chick that grew up in the hood, on a journey thru life as we all are, and telling my story and some of the testimonies of my Life of how I got to, "From Da Hood 2 Harvest". The Lord is so creative it makes me laugh sometimes, He gave me the name of this book one Sunday after church, I was sitting on my bed doing something and the Lord dropped it in my Spirit, and it just blew my mind. I started crying because he was dealing with me at the same time, it was a blessed overwhelming type of experience.

I was born in NC, but raised in Fayetteville NC, in one of the toughest and most drug infested hoods in this city at that time in the 1980s, 90s and thru the early 2000's. Back in the day, I ran tough and hard as a little girl to a young adult. But reading this book will tell how I almost did not make it out with my life. No one is perfect, but in this life, we have choices. There have been many words spoken over my life, some were bad, through pull down the witchcraft spirit that will try to put curses out to destroy my family and me. But God.

The prophecies that have been spoken over my life were awesome things that He is going to do in my life now and in the future. If I remain obedient, other things He has promise will come to pass. His timing is everything, I am patiently waiting.

I Made It
Out
Alive,
By the Grace of God

-Arry J. McNeill

The Beginning

To begin, my biological mom and I never really had a close relationship. It was just me and my little sister growing up in the home.

My mom was a single parent, she worked hard to make sure we had the main necessities to survive, but one of the major things she lacked was showing us that "MOTHERLY LOVE" that girls so desperately need especially when there is only one parent there to give it. She thought that as long as she is giving the financial part of it was good enough. She also had her nightlife as well.

My mother was a gambler, loved Bingo, Card-playing, and a functional alcoholic. Which also consumed most of her time and life, I guess you can say she tried to fit us in her life somewhere....When I was growing up, maybe around the age of 3 or 4, I guess my Dad didn't feel like we should be around my mom while she was living her life as she did. She loved to dance and drink. I assume that's where my sister and I got it from. So, he came to Raleigh NC to get me and my sister out of her care to bring us to Fayetteville to raise us up with a better life.

When he did that, I think that was the best thing, he could have ever done for me and my little sister. Between my grandfather and grandmother, which I called them Mom and Dad, they did everything in their power to give us the best life. When it came to my Dad, before we watch TV, went outside to play or do anything else, we had to get our education out the way first. From teaching us how to read, write, how to count, how to dress, how to cook, how to clean, shining his shoes, fixing a tie, ironing our clothes, fishing, hunting, reading the bible, praying, etc. My grandma gave us a choice in our learning activities. Our choices were learning to cook and bake, sewing, yarn crocheting, working in the garden and learning to plant, doing hair, making homemade ice cream, and how to be a respectable and biblical type of women. For myself, I chose to learn all of them, except crocheting, because in my mind, I thought to myself, look how awesome and amazing woman, mother, Woman of God, etc., my grandma was, So I wanted to be like her and have all those great qualities she had. As time passed, we are living our little lives traveling with them, going to church regularly, we were a Baptist family, and living the life of two little middle class spoiled colored girls. My Dad was an ordained Minister and Teacher of his Church, and he traveled extensively to various organized churches and meetings, teaching and ministering to people, giving communion, visiting the sick in the community. He was also a member of the different prestige community organizations, and much respect that he was a Retired Soldier from the Army. I loved to see my Dad in the podium speaking, it made me so proud of him to see how God would use him. I was honored to be his daughter. Even though he couldn't read well, his education was limited, but he helped his mother in the fields. Dad had so much wisdom and knowledge. Everyone loved him dearly. We always had company at the house. People drove miles away just to come and sit for hours and talk with him; it was the same way on his phone calls.

Around the age of seven or eight, my biological mother decided to move to Fayetteville as well and she wanted to get us back, but I didn't want to go with her. But she insisted, so at the beginning we went back and forth, but she still had the party thing going on, so she would go to work, get off from work and go hang out until late, and me and my little sister would either be home alone, or my grandparents would pick us up from school, and we would stay with them until she came and got us or we went to school from their house because she never came and picked us up. We lived in a two-bedroom apartment in a neighbor called Seabrook Hills. My mom was a hard worker in spite of everything, and kept the bills paid. I knew she loved us, but I don't think she knew how to show or give it. I'm sure it came from learned behavior from her mother. But most of all she was addicted to playing cards and gambling. So, we had card games and cookouts at our home every weekend. All the adults would be in the kitchen drinking, smoking, cursing, and wilding out. And the children would be playing videos games or either outside the running the neighborhood, playing kickball and other games, we had fun too. This went on most of my growing up. I remember one night she was having a game, and I and my little sister were in the bed sleeping, trying to sleep anyway thru the racket of the grow-ups partying in the kitchen.

I remember my first encounter with the devil. He was sitting beside my bed, I felt a weird feeling, so when I turned over and in disbelief of what I was really looking at. So, I turned over quickly in fear and closed my eyes as tightly as I could to make what I saw disappear. In my mind, laying there in fear, I said to myself let's try this again. So, I turned over again and the devil thing just stared at me again, so replayed it again and turns over for the last time but it was gone this time. I was thinking Praise God while shaking in fear. But my heart was still beating out my chest by that time, and I had to use the bathroom but was too scared to move. I never told anyone about it, because I was pretty sure no one was going to believe me anyways, until later as I got older and started going thru things and realized why he had visited me. He was letting me know I was up for a fight and he wanted me to see first -hand what and who I was dealing with. And the spiritual fight was on and popping shortly after....

Stolen Innocence

Around the age of 11, we were at another one of their card games at one of her friend girls, and that's where I was raped by one of her close friends son who was in his late teens, while they were in the front of the house playing cards. When I tried telling my mother about it, she didn't believe me, and told me I was probably being fast. After that it ripped my heart, that my mother would not believe that something so horrific had happen to her little baby girl and she didn't believe me, and why would I want to be raped like that, how could she be so cold to me? How could she not believe me? How could she not tell me to act on it or call the police? Why didn't she go to his mother and fight for me? That was the "FIRST SEED" that was planted. That was the first day that sparked my brokenness and broken heart…

Women who have had their innocence stolen from them are deeply torn and can mentally and emotionally affect us all through adulthood if we don't seek healing and deliverance. I received a lot of therapy as a youth to try to figure myself out after that happened to me. Most of the time we pack things on top of it and suppress the pain. Then we start dating or attracting certain type of men and don't even understand why.

The "Spirit of Perversion/Lust" is on us. We start acting out in many ways sexually, some women turn to homosexuality, some women turn to prostituting, some go to anything sexually that will feed that damage. That is why we have should seek professional and spiritual help. Jasmine Scurlock says, *"You can't heal, what you conceal".* So, making sure we are dealing with these demons is very vital. Let's say that you might be on your job or in the store, and you run into a young lady/man and you two start talking about the Lord.

From that conversation they began start sharing some private things about their past and you begin ministering to them. But it gets deep, and they get emotional and you begin praying with them. But then unexpectedly you start having flashbacks because you haven't dealt with your stuff properly. And you leave and get home and go into and deep depression or maybe even contemplate suicide. And that sexual feeling comes over you and you need that fix. But you are saved, and you thought you were doing ok. Then that reality check hits you. You know how I know it can happen because I dealt with some of these emotions. Sister I love you enough to say, if you are holding onto some of your past hurts, and you have some stuff packed away that you need to allow God to start cleaning out. It goes the same for the men as well. We hear a lot about pastors, coaches, etc.; because they were molested/raped as a child they end up doing the same to other little boys or girls. Therefore, because they never dealt with the tragedy, and now the Christian life is used to hide behind and try to cover it up. And we all know that has been a disaster for years. Let's pay attention and learn from others mistakes.

After you make the decision to give your life to Christ, these demons/spirits need to be renounced and to bind the strong man, which is binding the root of the demonic force. You can find more information about this from a book by Drs Jerry & Carol Robeson called Strongman's His Name, What's His Game; Spiritual Warfare. Just know the fight is a never ending process, continue to Fight.

As time passed, I began to be rebellious and hanging out in the streets doing things like selling drugs, smoking marijuana, drinking, and hanging out with older crowds. I tried to be the good daughter even though I was angry at her. In rebelliousness, I dyed that juicy jerry curl blonde anyways after she told me I couldn't. At that time, I had met this older boy and he said he wanted to be my boyfriend. So, I started being his girl, and right there is where another "SEED" was planted of being attracted to older men. It always starts with a seed, and then it will continue grow when it's fed anything close to what started it, whether it is good or bad.

Months later, I met his family and they loved me and took me in, and his mother is who dyed my hair for me. When my mom found out she was furious and tried to spank me and put me on punishment. We argued and I ran away for the first time, and I did this repeatedly thereafter. From my perspective, the relationship between Helen and I was over. I started staying with him and his family and then he changed and started beating on me and making me do things with him, and when I didn't do them, he would beat me or choke me for it. That lasted for a while and then I ran away from his house and came back home to Helen and then he came looking for me and wouldn't leave me alone and he tried to fight on me one day and I told my cousins and they threatened him, and I ran off from him, and I didn't have to worry about him anymore.

The Move

When I turned 13 years of age, and my little sister was 11 years of age, we then moved to this dead-end street full of everything, and at the time, I didn't know that another part of my life was about to get real for me. When we got acquainted and settled that's when I started exploring the hood and the area meeting new people. That's when I meet my first street family, they accepted me just the way I was. I learned everything I needed to learn to survive "The Life in the Hood."

I learned how to do everything pertaining to it, to sale drugs, and hanging out in the streets etc. That's when I really started getting in trouble, fighting, getting suspended all the time, skipping school, drinking and smoking weed was my thing, and I learned about clubbing, I started going and partying all time. This is around the time when "Clarissa" came about and was created as my other personality. Yes honey, watch out now, she was ready for the world.

Like Beyoncé' and Sasha fierce. I started acting out more and more. I always had a sassy, strong attitude anyways. My mother always had to pop me in my mouth, because I was too outspoken. I had an aggressive attitude and temper as well. Too much at my age I might say. Maybe it was passed down, my dad always said I reminded him of his mom, whom I was also named after. My anger grew worse, and my attitude got stronger. I started staying out all the time and skipping school to hang out. I was in middle school, getting in trouble at school, and my mom had to come there often because of my aggressive behavior.

I first met the Kirdinski family on the street, and then some others that took me in as their own. It felt good to be loved and accepted, I wasn't used to all this, this one little street and all this family love. Then I met another new family, the Swaheli's, and they accepted me in like one of their own as well, and my childhood Best friend, which we are today still holding strong, and very dear to my heart. In those days it was safe to hang out in the streets all night and go to house parties, clubs, after hour liquor houses, etc. And when I say I partied like no other with my girl at the time. Man, we partied and had a ball. Those were the good old days. My homegirl I hung out with joined me and we went to all the hottest clubs in the city, and all the strip bars where they had all the big ballers from everywhere. We always had a blast, and we partied all night until the sun came up.

The Mental Break

I guess I was around the age 14 or 15 when I experienced my first breakdown. I guess everything finally caught up to me. I found out that you drink and party your problems away. One day it had to have been on a Saturday, because on Saturdays was always cleaning up days in our household. My mom must have told us to get the house together. I was being rebellious and told her I wasn't doing anything, I then told her that my sister Rubbia had to do the kitchen since she wasn't doing anything. We begin to argue; I got so angry at her that I went to get a knife out the sink and came at her. I guess my mom said that was the last straw. My hurt and anger turned into violence. The next thing I know is my mother woke me up one day and told me to pack my bags, and then she took me to this place that looked like a business building, I thought it was a group home at first, and I had to talk to these people. This man called me in the office and started asking me all these questions and showing me, all these pictures asking me what they are, so I answered his questions. He leaves out to go speak to mom. The next thing I know they are telling me to get my things and taking me thru these double doors and introducing me to the staff and showing me my room. I then realized that my mom had admitted me into a mental/behavioral facility. I thought to myself, I know this heffa did not do this to me. I was really furious with Helena at that point, but it was nothing I can do about it now, so I just had to deal with it, for now. Feel me! So, I ended up staying there about 8 or 9 months. I learned a lot while locked up in that place, we had to go group sessions, medication management, we were still able to go to school, they transferred our records from public, we went on field trips, and did some things as public school just in a locked down facility. But as time passed, I met a lot of teenagers from all over, with all kinds of life stories, with their own issues like mine or maybe even worse. Sadly, I went through a few things in there, like getting into fights, prejudice, but I made it through, and I learned a lot in that journey as well.

Note: We don't realize that some of the things we do in our lives and the decisions we made, even

being parents, caused generation curses to come upon us and our children and could be passed down. Certain lifestyles we live and participate in, behaviors, environments, causes an open door to different spirits to come in. *The Enemy loves to keep us in the dark and spiritually uneducated to his tactics and works. (Hosea 4:6)*

Returning Home

After making it back home and getting settled back in school, one day I met who is now my two daughter's father, a tall and handsome New Orleans Boy named Dan but we called him Dee, who was different from the regular guys that I was used to, and I liked that about him, he was the new guy on the block as we called it. We started dating in the 7th grade, and we fell in love, at least I thought it was love at that age. He started doing things for me, buying me jewelry, clothes, and shoes, took me out, he spoiled me all the time. He was my first D-Boy at a young age. We started being together all the time, skipping school and doing everything together. Then he took me to meet his family, the Thompkins, and they loved me for me, and I became a part of their family too. I was so happy and loved them too. Mostly because I didn't have a relationship with my own mom. He said his mom was a Christian lady, since I was with them all the time, she started taking me to church with her. I started learning different things about the Bible, God and Jesus Christ in a different way. It was sure what I learned from the Baptist church I grew up in. I really liked that House of God. It's where I was baptized, got saved, and received the Holy Spirit as a teenager. But sad to say I didn't realize I wasn't finished with Worldly Life either. (James 1:8)

True Monster Inside

As time went on one day Dee changed, he saw me talking to one of my homeboys in one of our local projects where they lived. He waited until he got me in the back of one of the apartments, and ask me what I was doing, and I told him I was talking to one of our friends from school, and he slapped me so hard in the face, he made me stagger. When I realized what had happened, I took off running and crying as fast as I could to get away from him, until I got to safety. I ran straight through the back door of his mother house, praying that the door was unlock so he couldn't catch me and hit me again, and his mother was in the kitchen yelling and asking me what is wrong? She turned and look at him as he came dashing in 100 miles per hour behind me, what did you do to this girl? I told her he hit me, and she got on him. But I promise you he didn't listen, because after that day, I met the "TRUE MONSTER INSIDE" … I constantly dealt with his verbal, physical abuse, and control; I even had to walk with my head down when I was around other men, so I wouldn't get accused of anything because of his insecurities. If I did, I sure was going to pay for it later. I had to fight for my life during those times. Dealing with the stalking and fear of my life to be anywhere because I knew he would probably show up there and try to fight on me. No matter where I was, I could never hide from him. It was like he was physic or something. Sometimes, I really think the devil was telling him where I was. That might sound crazy to you; let me tell you one thing, the devil has power too. He has a score to settle with God and he is very angry, because when he was put out of Heaven with the third of the angels, it has become his mission to keep us out of Heaven as well. He is the "god of this world" so who ever gives him power over their life, he will activate himself and live in them and have power over their minds and bodies. He is after the Our Soul, that's the **ONLY** thing he wants from us. So, I believe he allowed the enemy to have control over him at some point. When we were together, I would always see dark images around or following us or standing at the windows. I will tell you one time we were sleeping, and I woke up and saw the grim-reaper standing at our room door. I could have used the bathroom on myself that's how scared I was. When I woke him up to tell him he said that was not the first time. I'm like dude death is following you around and you acting like you are not worried. I just shook my head and started praying for him and us. Then as time passed, we were going through middle school onto high school in our relationship with the abuse worsening. At the age 17 years old, I became pregnant with my first daughter on my 18th birthday, we have the same birthday, I had my second daughter at the age 19 years old. I was abused all through my pregnancies and after which caused a lot of bodily damage that I encountered. This was the beginning of being a single mother. He used to make me have sex with him and force me to give him oral sex, I cried the whole time, even when I refused to do what he asked, He beat me senseless and sometimes until I was unconscious. Like, the time when we got into an argument because I wanted to leave him and go home, he beat me with bed boards, until my legs turned purple and clumpy, and then he busted me over the head with the large pickle jar. When I woke up, I was on his mother hallway floor because I was tired of the abuse, secrets and the lies. Another incident was we were sitting in the living at his friend house, and I was trying to leave him again, he said ok, and told me that I could leave, I get up to get ready to walk out the door with my bags, and he pulls this two-barrel shot gun from under the couch and unlocked the door for me, cocked the gun back and said leave then! I looked at him like he was crazy like really dude, fear came over my body and tears just ran down my face, because I just knew I was I going to die that day just because I wanted to be free. Now I understood what those people back in the day went through just for freedom and to be released from slavery. Because I was in slavery to a Monster, of Abuse and Anger, and bondage of the man that I loved very much, who fathered my children. I loved him and wanted him to change so we could be together living happily ever after raising our girls. So, knowing that he was very serious and capable of doing exactly that which is killing me so that no one will have me. The tattoo he had put on his chest with an Oozy and my name under it assured me of that. I then sat down on the couch and just cried for hours and prayed to God that I was so tired of this life, and I wanted out. And he said, "I THOUGHT SO", and he went back to playing the PlayStation game with an evil smirk on his face. Another time, I can remember another time when Dee dragged me through the woods of Shaw road because of his jealousy. He had me in the back of this wooded area, threw me on the ground and started beating me repeatedly. He sat on top of me and just kept punching me repeatedly in the face and everywhere. He had his hands around my throat choking me and slapping me. I was trying my best to fight him off, but of course he was stronger than me. I just kept begging him to stop and let me go, and he just kept going with the fear that I could possibly die that day. The excruciating pain I was feeling from every fist blow, and then he picked up a board he found that had nails in it and started hitting me with that too. With the last little bit of breath, I had in me, I screamed out and said JESUS HELP ME, HELP ME JESUS PLEASE HELP ME, I was just crying and screaming. and he said in this real deep and demonic voice, "YOU ARE GOING TO DIE TODAY", AND called me a female dog. Then suddenly, this car pulled up out of nowhere with its lights gleamed on us, He said to him, what is going on? What are you doing? Get off her and let her go, I got up and ran to the car and jumped in, with blood flowing down from all my wounds, and he split my right ear from the first punch to my head. Lord I thank God for saving me. Lord, I just want to thank for your hand being over my life. Another time when he chased me through the railroad tracks of Hillsboro street, under the bridge, and one the ladies off my street was walking thru the path to get home, which I thank God for even to this day, because he was about to put a whooping on me for whatever pissed him off that day. The lady said, "LET HER GO NOW!" He yelled back at her and told her to mind her own business with some ugly words involved. But he kept right on beating me. She yelled again and told him to let me go, "HE SAID AGAIN MIND YOU BUSINESS BEFORE I DO THE SAME THING TO YOU", and she told him, 'If you try it I will kill you myself", by then she started walking towards us down the railroad tracks and she had this look on her face that she meant everything she said to him. By that time, I had tussled my way free and ran to Ms. Kurtskin house, my God-mom house, crying and choking and I banged on the door, she opened, and I told her what happened. When she saw him coming up the street after me, she came out on the porch with her gun pointed at him and told him if he didn't leave, she would shoot him, and trust me, she meant it. She kept the gun on him, so he didn't take her for a joke. Then she told him she better not ever hear of him putting his hands on me again. And he finally left, and I decided to stay at her house for a while until I felt safe and comfortable enough to leave and go home.

From being beat with boards, busted over the head with jars, blackouts from the pain, left in the woods for dead, my ear getting split in half from the impacts of his fist, shotguns put to my head, being tortured for days, and damaged bones, being followed by death spirits. With me being such a young girl having to endure such horrific and painful and dangerous love from another human being. But God once again heard my cry for deliverance and rescued me.

A Lost to Gun Violence

On August 26, 1997, my daughters father lost his life to senseless gun violence due to retaliation, he was shot with a 25' millimeter, and the bullet that entered his side ricocheted through his body and tore all his main arteries and caused him to bleed internally. And to say he didn't get a chance to see his daughters grow up and get to see how wonderful, talented, creative, smart, and beautiful young ladies they have become. He would have been so proud. The time before this happened to him God showed it to me in a dream. God usually deals with me in dreams. In the dream, I was walking down the street with my oldest daughter in my arms and this red car was coming towards me getting ready to pull up to me but then guns came out of nowhere and they were getting ready to shoot but I woke up. God showed me what was going to happen before it happened, but I didn't know it was my girl's father it was going to be him. Because I had completely stopped dealing with him after the last incident, he was still allowed to see his girls, but could not take them with him. That day before everything transpired, I received word that he had went by the Daycare to see them and spend time with them. That night we were at my mom house, suddenly, my oldest daughter just started screaming and crying. I usually could get her to calm down, because she was never a cry baby like my baby girl was. She was a talker ever since she was about 6mths old. But then I received a phone call that he was shot and rushed to the hospital. At that moment is when I knew that she felt something happened to her daddy. We met the family at the hospital, now that was heart-breaking because as mean and horrible as he was to me, I never wanted anything bad to happen to him, I wanted God to fix him and change him, so we could be one big happy family, us and his girls. As we all know God, most of the time has a different plan than ours. While in the waiting room, we just kept praying and praying for him while the doctors were doing their best to work on him. His mother let out this cry and said to me what if he doesn't want to live, and I just looked at her in confusion. I'm thinking in my mind like of course he wants to live, he wants to see his girls who he adored so much, he named them both at birth. But I just kept praying for him. Some time passed, and the doctors came out to talk to us, and they gave us the worse news of our lives, **'WE ARE SORRY MAM, WE DID EVERYTHING WE COULD, HE DIDN'T MAKE IT"**

His mom just wailed so loud, the sound that came from her body was horrific. They told us that they were going to clean him up and let us go back to see him before they take him to the morgue. We went back to see him, and he was just lying there on that cold, hard table lifeless. We all had our moments and said our last words, but when his little cousin (R.I.H. Josh) went to him, it's like he went into a twilight zone. When he snapped back into it, he told us that Danny spirit spoke to him, and said he sat on the side of the table, and "told him to tell everyone to not retaliate, that God was going to bring justice." And told him to give me a message as well. And God kept his word the guy turned himself in to authorities and was charged for his murder. I went through a long depression stage after that, trying to find myself again from all the mental damage and I had to get my identity back. I also put the oldest child in therapy at 2 years old because she started acting out and being mean. I never thought I would have to raise my girls alone, But I guess it was God's will. God healed me and kept me through it.

THE DEADLY SHOOT-OUT

In September 1997, my home girl, family and myself were at home this night. We were getting ready to get dressed to go out to the strip club where one of my friends worked at night. She wanted to let us to see what it was like to be a dancer. I wondered what it was like, but I assumed God would not be pleased with that idea at all. This was another one of the scariest days of my life. On this day, our home was shot up, I was shot in the head, At the time I was on the phone, at first I didn't even know I was shot until a few minutes later when I felt something wet running down the back of my neck, then down my shoulder to the front of my shirt, and then I realized it was blood, and then I panicked. The crazy thing is while that was happening, bullets were still flying through the house like World War II, and I must have been in shock for a second, but then something snapped my mind back to reality to what was really going and that was somebody could die tonight.

BUT GOD!! He saved me again, he spared all of us for that matter, and my home girl was shot in the foot, to take the bullet for my second baby girl as she snatches her up from all the flying bullets shifting through the house like an action movie. I called 911. As we were hiding in the back of the house, praying and waiting, and waiting for the guns to stop roaring, and waiting for the police to show up. I later found out that there were 187 or more rounds that were let off. And none of us died!! Can you believe that? None of us died…

Wow! God is a Protector and his grace and mercy rested on us that night. I was supposed to be dead and I'm pretty sure a closed casket too. If it was up to the Enemy, we were all supposed to be dead. Then all our souls would have been lost. No chance to repent, get saved or nothing. I'm sure that was the devils plan. Really, a bullet to the back of the head and it ricochet from the ceiling to my head and all it did was split my head, which left a large gash and we left the hospital with just stitches and bandages. Still to this day, I rub my hand across my scar, especially when it rains, and say, NOTHING BUT THE MERCY AND THE LOVE OF GOD FOR US!!

The next day or so, I received a phone call from my auntie, she explained she heard the news of what happened. She said she was at prayer service that night and the Lord put me in her spirit, and she started saying, "THE BLOOD THAT COVERETH, THE BLOOD THAT COVERETH". She was interceding for poor little me. Lord I thank the Lord for her being obedient, because the product of it all is me sitting here writing to tell about it. Thank you, Auntie, I Love You So Dearly. You don't even know. Let me explain something to you all when prayer is involved it makes all the difference in your life.

If you don't have an active prayer life or around someone who you know can get a prayer through, you better get you one. We have time and give time to everything else, partying, boyfriends, girlfriends, sex, traveling, work, money, etc. But we forget about God, the Word of God, our spiritual life, and where our souls are going to spend eternity. You're your account full & active because your Soul depends on it.

LIFE AFTER THE SHOOT-OUT

The following year, on June 1998, I gave birth to my third child which was my first son. Raising my children as a single mother was one of the most challenging oppositions in my life. But remembering all the things my dad taught me growing up, giving up was never an option. But getting a plan to make it happen was and praying to God to help me through it all. As time passed, I decided to go back to school, so I would have more than just the title "single mom" or being a guy "baby-momma" I started attending at a local community college for my Associates degree in Human Services. I have been blessed with the heart of giving and helping, which entails many things, so I decided to go into a field that could help produce those things and be effective to my community, plus watching my parents because they were getting older and a little sick. Along with doing that, I also worked full-time job as a Manager, along with that I was taking care of my grandma while she was sick. So, I put my children in one of the most wonderful daycares in Fayetteville at that time to care for my children while I was being the black "WONDERWOMAN" pursuing my dreams and taking care of my family. I strived to give my children everything they deserved in life, I figured just because I didn't have a man or their dad in our lives to complete us, doesn't mean they didn't deserve the best things in Life. I told myself that I would not "BE BITTER, JUST BETTER". Forgive and move on, because the forgiving part is not for them, it is for me, and God will handle the rest, if we let him. (Matt. 6:14-15). I had enough faith, and the prayers I prayed, that God would be there for me and bless us. After everything I had already been through my faith was increased and I couldn't disappoint him in all he brought me through. As I continued to work hard, going to church, going to school, trying to live own my on, I still faced a lot of challenges, But I never gave up, did I feel like it sometimes? of course, but if I gave up, how would I be able to help someone else, and be able to encourage them, that they can do it as well?

Deadly Argument

In May 2008, was another one of the worst days of my life. My boyfriend and I, at the time got into an altercation because I caught him cheating again with the same female we had been going back and forth about for years. Just to give a brief history on that relationship. We had had a heck of a relationship. What we had was called "Dangerous Love", ya'll know that song by Destiny Child. We used to club together, fight together, drink together, smoke together, we tried X-Pills together, those altering attitude/behavior drugs do it every time. We were always in court for domestic disputes; I guess you can say we were a wild couple. I think I was way out my element this time. On this night, this argument didn't end as the others. I pulled up to see him with this chick again, and we all argued as usual, she gets in her car and tries to run me over with her car multiple times while yelling out the window, but my attention went back on him as we are arguing. I must have blacked out because I don't remember anything until I heard the ambulance. I realized then I did something very bad. I went home and kissed my children and called my family. Next thing I know, I was being handcuffed in front of my children and taken to jail. One thing I have learned in this life is this; Hurt people always hurt people in man forms physically, mentally, or emotionally.

Jail Time

As I sat in jail, God dealt with me like never before. If anyone one of you ever have a real relationship with God, and he has his hands upon your life, he chastises those who belongs to him. (Heb. 12:6) And Lord knows he did. I didn't get any rest the whole time I was incarcerated. As that young man lay up in the hospital fighting for his life. I was charged with three different charges of assault, which one of them would be a felony, the DA was trying to send me up the river. But God had a different plan for Arry Jay. The next day the jail minsters came in to talk to us. I tried to hide because I saw one of the ladies that knew my Dad. I tried to hurry up and hide back in my cell, I was so ashamed. But she spotted me anyway. I think God set it up like that. She started talking to me, and she said I don't want to know what you did, because the Lord knows, I am just going to read the Word to you, as she did, I just sat there with my head down, listening and being convicted. After she finished reading, she asked did I want to give my life to Christ, I just looked at her confused, but I accepted, and gave my life back to Christ that day. She gave me the tightest hug of Love. It blessed me. I couldn't understand that she was showing me so much love and not judging me. She was just doing the will of her Father. While I was in Jail, God sent this Preacher lady in there to speak to me while I was in one of the group sessions they have for the inmates. On this day we had group, we were talking about REJECTION, and in the middle of the group the preacher lady looks at me and says, "GOD SAID YOU WILL NOT FALL AGAIN", and I just looked at her in confusion like what in the world! But she said it again "GOD SAID YOU WILL NOT FALL AGAIN", "GOD SAID YOU MUST PUT HIM FIRST, MY KIDS SECOND, AND EVERYTHING ELSE AFTER", "AND THAT HE WAS GOING TO WORK THIS OUT AND THIS WILL BE LAST TIME I FALL" BUT I MUST BE OBEDIENT! Tears just started flowing down my face and I got chills all over my body, as I am getting now as I'm writing this. Every time I tell this testimony of how awesome, real and faithful God is. After the group, I went back to my cell, got on my knees, praying and thanking him for coming to see about me. Because I just knew after I have done this God was done with me. Even in this God loved me. (Jer. 31:3) The blessing in all this, the young man Lived and decided not to press charges against me. The next week or so after that incident, I was released from jail. I kissed the ground and I walked all the way to my sister house. After all that I didn't want to be in anything closed in, forget that. I went to court and the favor of God was on my life, my name was called to appear before the judge, he read my charges out, the DA said some things, the judge asked me some questions, he said who is here with you today, I told him my mom, my sister and my babies. He got quiet for a minute. He then proceeded to say that we are going to dismiss all the other charges, and drop these charges down to misdemeanors except one, that will be held a felony. Then he says there will be no courts cost or fees, one year of probation, and assigned me to probation officer that was there in court, and said YOU ARE FREE TO GO!! Do you understand where my mindset was, I was baffled, I was in shock in what God had done in that court room. I grabbed my babies and I hugged and kissed them and my family as we left. When I got home, I praised God all over that house. I felt like David in the Bible when he danced out of his clothes.

New Beginnings

I decided to enroll in College, focus on God and my family, and show my kids that I can do better. So, I did just that. I will tell you another testimony, because of my past, and my record, I had to see the Dean of the Program I was registered in, and they had to make the decision of me entering the Major I chose. But with a lot of Prayer and Faith, and God's favor, he touched the Dean heart, and she decided to give a chance and let me in. Lord, I just want to thank you. My heart was so over joyed. So, I went straight to work, and worked hard. It was not easy. I was a single mother of four young children, working full-time, my boys were in different activities, and I was helping my parents. But I prayed all the time for God to give me the strength to carry me through it all. Once again God was so faithful, and he did it.

Good-Bye Grandma & Grandpa

In 2009, my grandma, the woman who raised me; I called her mom, became sick and passed away. that broke my heart so bad, that lady taught me almost everything I know. In 2011, my dad died from Pneumonia, now that was the toughest, everyone in my family thought this was going to take me out.

They were so worried about me, because he was my heart. When Dad was in the hospital, the nurses notified us that he would not live much longer to live, because his lungs was full of infection from the pneumonia. I knew my Dad was a strong man, and a fighter; he didn't want to let go for our sake. Most of the time, he worried about the kids and I. Man! he sure loved them kids dearly. At that time everyone went to his hospital bed side and said their heartfelt words. Of course, I was the last one to go up; I had to prepare my mind and my life with the reality that we might not have him around anymore. So, when it was time to go to his bed side, one of the ladies from his church, a very close friend of the family, that knew me my whole life, pulled me to the side and gave me a heartfelt talk. My Dad was holding on, knowing that I have to let go, so he will let go. I heard them tell me that the nurses are waiting for me to give them the ok to turn the machines off, but I couldn't do it, I just couldn't do it. It hurt me to see him hurting and fighting for his life while in pain. The machine was pumping so hard to get the infection out of him, but it wasn't enough. I'm sure his body was tired of all the pulling, poking, and machines. The time came when I got the heart to go to him. I climb in the bed with him and put my arms around his frail body, then poured my heart and soul out to him, hoping he can hear me; letting him know that "God was going to take care of the kids as well as me. I told him we will be fine. I thanked him for being so good to us. I finally thank him for being an amazing example, father, Man of God and demonstrating the Love of God. I reminded him of how he raised us, the good old days. What memories it will be. At that moment I couldn't understand why he had to leave us; but I knew it was the Lord's will. I love you so much Daddy. I understood that Dad completed his earthly purpose. Afterwards, I just cried and cried, as the nurses proceeded to pull the plug on the machines, and it felt like my life was drifting away with his last breaths. After he went to be with the Lord, I continued to lay there in the hospital bed with him until my Family said Arry you must get up and let them take him. We left the Hospital and the reality of life without my dad was smacking me in the face. As I am sitting here writing this, I can't even remember the wake before the funeral, I guess I blocked it out, that was my traumatic experience I assume. Because he was so loved we had to have two funeral services for him, one at the church we grew up in, and the other service in our home town in Piney Grove, Maxton. Where we laid his body to rest with the other family. The Once again had begun, Lord knows it was so hard; I started therapy for a while to get through the grieving process. But with God holding me up, I knew we all were going to make it. My kids were hurt about losing grandpa. He had them so spoiled, and they loved going over his house and staying for days. So many great memories. God is a Healer, and I knew that if He carried us through all the other traumatic situations that happened in my life; that he would carry me through this too. I do believe what doesn't kill you, will make you stronger. I look at myself in the mirror and shake my head and say Arry Jay girl it had to be the Lord strength.

Back to College Decisions

Despite the odds, of my past mishaps, the grace and favor of God on my life; here I am a single mom of for children, working full time, weekly classes, and caring for other family member, and a devastating divorced, having to take a semester off due to everything going on, starting my life over less than a year, after I got married, having a nervous break-down, started having stress & anxiety attacks, all within the 4 ½ years in school, but on May 8, 2017 I walked across the stage with my Bachelors in Social Work. To God Be the Glory. My God!! My God!! Wont He do It!! Yes, He Will!! I'm telling you, please don't give up! No matter what is going on in your life, if you have the Lord on your side, I promise you that anything and all things are all possible with Jesus Christ. Now what if I would have just thrown my hands up in the midst of these storms? I wouldn't be writing this book to let you know that I was more than a Conqueror through Christ Jesus. I'm a living testimony that it can be done. As time passed, I learned that I was Called and Chosen for this, and that this journey was not only for me, but I had to go through this Journey for you all (Rom. 8:37).

Journey Scriptures

Matthew 22:14- "For many are called, but few are Chosen".

Ephesians 4:1-According as he hath chosen us, in Him before the foundation of the World, that we be holy and without blame before him in Love".

Jer. 1:5- "Before I formed thee in the belly, I knew thee; and before thou camest forth out of the womb I sanctified thee, and I ordained thee a prophet unto the nations".

Meeting Mr. Right

In 2012, I met this guy, that I used to know from junior high, he said he saw me on social media, and reached out to me. We haven't seen each other in ages. I was cordial; we chopped it up a little, and kept it moving. Some time passed he reached out to me again, we were talking about how he had a crush on me in school. I was with my girls Dad in junior high, and that's part of why he used to bully me. Honestly, I really wasn't interested. I was in my own world enjoying my single life, and my babies. I was at the point where I didn't trust men anymore. He finally asked me on a date, eventually I decided to go. We dated for a short period, and he asked me to be his lady, his words were, "the last time I waited I lost, and it took 20 years to find you again, so I have to move quick, so I don't lose you again". So, I accepted, we were now in a relationship. As time went on, I finally let him meet my children, I assumed they liked him. They got along well. I met his family, they loved me. I loved his mother and she was so sweet. We talked about everything. Then he moved in with us. And shortly after he asked me to marry him, and I obliged. Unfortunately, while we were engaged, I found out that he was surfing the web for women, and one of his ex-girlfriends reached out to me to inform me some things about Mr. Slick-Rick/Wrong. I guess I needed to find him out for myself, that's usually how some of us women are about our men. You know how we are as woman thinking the ex, a woman scorned, is hating on us and playing get back, but I didn't totally disregard her information either. I sure wished, I would I have paid attention to those red flags. So, I made me a fake page on the dating website, I discovered he was using. To find out if the man that I was going to marry was cheating on me. But I stayed to see maybe he would change or maybe it was just a phase. I kept my incognito with my identity for some time and he went along with and he disclosed that he was getting married soon but wanted a friend. So, I went along with it for as long as I could to see if this negro was going to come to his senses and get right, he didn't. By this time, we were supposed to meet up, but I just got so angry and blew my cover. And went off on him and told him it was me he was going to meet that day, and I was going to leave him because I couldn't believe that he was doing that to us. Let me tell you something ladies, one thing I have learned about a man, that you better "PAY ATTENTION TO THE SIGNS" …

It will save you a lot hurt, time, and money at the beginning. There are always signs men give you that they are who they are. They might be a good man, but are they good for you? These are some questions you should always ask yourself and seek God and wait it out.

Should I accept this? Do I have to accept this? Do I deserve more than this? The #1 question is he "SAVED?" #2 "DOES HE HAVE A PERSONAL RELATIONSHIP WITH GOD?" Because, if he does not have one, he does not know who he is. God gives identity. We must seek God for our Identity. If God doesn't change him or grooms his heart with love, WOMAN YOU CAN'T CHANGE HIM, YOU WILL ONLY BE RAISING HIM ALL OVER AGAIN!! But I gave him another chance, but he had to delete that page and any other pages he had and promise me he would be faithful and honest from here on out. In 2013, we got married, we had a beautiful wedding, and our lives together were to begin. I have also learned over the years that if a man has not yet dealt with things in his past and childhood, and found healing, therapy or even deliverance for them. Unfortunately, You will most likely face issues in the relationship/marriage. There is a hole in the soul, that only God the divine healer can fill & fix. He is the only POTTER; we are the clay.

Mr. Wrong & The Mask

Now I am Mrs. Macnezy, to the man I'm supposed to spend the rest of my life with, but he has changed suddenly. Women, some men are capable to present themselves as whoever and whatever we want them to be, because we share so much of our emotions and our heart with them too early in the meeting and dating phase. They just go along with it because of their hidden agendas from the start. We give them the hand to play us with and we don't even know it. Then when they get what want from us. We are so hurt and devastated, looking like a deer caught in headlights; confused. So, we need to learn to listen and watch them more closely and definitely listen to the small still voice of God and signs He gives us to be aware of what and who we are getting ourselves involved with. But we are already married now, because I loved him and I'm thinking maybe it's just the newlywed jitters or something. I just knew this was the man that God has sent me, and I was so happy. It had to be right, we got married in a church, he wasn't saved though, but I was. He started going to church with me at first then he just completely stopped. But I had to stay prayerful and positive. But oh well, it was a long day, the family did have a little after party after everything. Things were going ok in the house, I guess. I was told the first year is kind of rough so just go along with and continue to pray for my family and marriage, as I did. I always tried to be the peace maker. In September of the following year, we went on the honeymoon, and it was such an amazing trip to New York. My husband put me in a horse & carriage ride through central park, roses and gifts, shopping, and most of all I got to meet my new family. Everyone that knows me knows that I love family and that's one thing that is always dear to my heart. It was time for me to make it back home. A few weeks went by and I was informed from my children that they think that he was doing something, that I should check it out. They told me that they had known for a while but was scared to tell me because of me being happy; they didn't want to hurt me. But they couldn't take it anymore. So, with the information they shared with me I just held on to it and just did my research, and my investigation, before I went to him with the evidence. Because of the type of person, he was you had to have cold hard evidence for him, and put it in front of him, and even with that the crazy fool would still lie, and say it wasn't him, just to cover himself. Lord I was dealing with a major narcissistic personality man. Trust me it was crazy.

News Concerning Mother

But sadly, I had to take a break from the Husband distrust and my investigation, because I received the phone call from my sister that my mom had fallen, and broken her Femur bone, and was rushed to the hospital. We all met her up there to make sure she was going to be ok. Of course, we knew she would, she had retired from there a few years prior. My mom was a former employee there for over 25 years, she had just retired few years before. She then started living her best life. I loved seeing her happy and having fun with her new friends.

Instead, now she is laying in a hospital bed preparing for surgery. She was off to surgery, after some time the doctor came out to speak us about her surgery, the doctor informed us that while he was trying to fix her femur, he found cancer, and that was the cause of her breakage. The doctor came out to talk to us after her surgery. He explained to us that they found cancer in her bone, that's why her femur broke, he was spreading to her lungs, her kidneys, and it was spreading quickly thru out her whole body, it's one of the most progressive cancer he had seen in a long time. So, he was going to set up physical therapy after her surgery to get her back moving around. So, we had planned to move her in with us until she was healthy enough to be on her own again. All this happened on a Saturday. By Tuesday, the doctors had her on a breathing machine. I know she tried to be strong, I also knew she was scared. I think she knew that she was sick way before this situation occurred and she kept it to herself so she wouldn't worry the family. I was already praying for her, by that Thursday I could see the fear in her eyes, and I just grabbed her hands and started praying for her, and tears started flowing down her face. Her hospital friends and co-workers kept her busy with visits and flowers, when we were at work. The doctor put on her on the breathing machine because the doctor said that the cancer was wrapping itself around her lungs like an Octopus, and that is what was making it hard for her to breath. He said that she will be fine if the medication continues to work for her.

On that following Saturday morning, I was work and I got the call the family needed to get to the hospital as soon as possible. My mom had made a turn for the worst. We all made it up to the hospital and met with the doctors. They told us that the cancer had spread through her whole body and that she wasn't going to make it through the day. But I just kept praying and praying. We still felt the need to call everyone to let them know so they could come see her before God calls her home if that was His will. I am thankful that the Lord let her stay with us a little longer. That Sunday morning, I got a call from my sister saying I need to get to the hospital as fast as I could because she did not know it was not going to be much longer, plus the nurse said she kept taking her breathing mask off her face, and my sister kept putting it back on. The family and I jumped up and made our way to the hospital, we arrived, jumped on the elevator, we ran down the hall and pushed the room door open and looked at my sister sitting by her side, with my mom, we were too late she had passed away while my sister was sitting next her bed, sleeping beside her. I just screamed and became nauseated and fell to the floor, NOOOO MOMMA, OMG NO MOMMA, LORD MY MOMMA GONE! On November 19, 2013 my mom transitioned to her heavenly home. I'm feeling so lost now, I have lost my grandmother, that I called momma, the woman that raised and taught me almost everything I know. I have lost the man that raised me, I called Dad, the only man that I had in my life. Now my Mom…Oh yes, now this is too much for me. I'm feeling empty. I started to slip into another state of depression. The night before she passed I had this weird dream, that I went to the hospital to see her, but when I got there we went outside to the top of the hospital and set up lawn chairs like we were at the beach and the sun was shining on us so beautiful, it was like the sunset on the beach.

And I looked at her and I asked her, Are you ok, ma? She said I'm fine. She was just sitting in the chair looking at the sky like she was looking at someone talking to her. And the dream just drifted away very softly, and I woke up crying. Maybe that was my sign right there, but I just didn't want to accept it. We had her Funeral, all the kids took it hard, just like they did after losing their other grandparents. I went to church that following Sunday and I was still grieving, my pastor did an altar call for anyone who desired prayer. I felt the need to go up and get some much-needed prayer. As I was getting prayed for, I could feel the Lord wrapping his arms around me, and then I went into the spirit and saw my mom and said, "I'm ok, don't worry about me." And I just passed out on the floor just crying my eyes out. But I could hear the preacher saying just leave her there The Lord is working on her. I wasn't the same when I got up. Once again, I thank the Lord for being a healer. If you just surrender it all to him, HE WILL MAKE YOU WHOLE. (Psalms 147:3)

Note Of Encouragement

To the Women, the struggles we are facing today in our lives are not to show us how weak we are, but to bring out the power that you hold on the inside through Him.

God is trying to develop you into what you were created to do and be the strong and empowered Woman of God he purposed in you. Your obstacles are not to drown you, but to teach you how to sustain and persevere through the struggles and pressures of this life. (Eph. 6:18)

In Standing, I have learned how to rise above the waves and see myself in who He called me to be. I've learned to use the very strength that He has given me. You can only get things from the Heavenly Father. I encourage you that when you have done all you can, continue to hold on to His Word, and still STAND. (Eph. 6:13-14)

God is stretching us, to pull the things out of us that is needed for our Christian walk. The stretching and pulling is to push us into maturity and growth in Him. It causes us to pray more, stay in our word and seek wisdom, understanding, and revelation from the Lord. (Prov. 4:7)

With our growth things of this world should not move us, because we are so focused on Him that we believe what His word tells us. We should be better than where we are. We have wasted so much time playing church, when we are the church and people should look at us and desire the Holy Spirit we have. We as Children of God should continuously hunger and thirst after his righteousness daily. It is so much compromising going in the churches nowadays just to keep the member rosters up or the pockets fat, no one wants to live Holy anymore. Holiness is a lifestyle and it still matters People of God. The church standards have fallen off. And God is not pleased with any of it. It is too much learned behavior and having the form of Godliness and deny the power going on. I believe at some point we all need to sit down and be re-taught over again and allow God to break us down so we can really be used by him. Because if the Body of Christ as a whole doesn't get it together soon. **HELL IS ITS HOME!!**

No Exceptions or No Exemptions. Forget these title, Bishop this, Apostle this, and Pastor that, and Prophet(tess) this, and Doctor this and reverend that, forget those titles and degrees, those fancy expensive robes with all the fancy stuff on it to make you feel like somebody, forget that thousand dollar or million dollar buildings, If God puts prophetic calling on your life, remember you did not give it to yourself that you think you gave to yourself, and fire anointing that makes you think you are better than anyone in the church or your family, Leaders teaching what they think, or what they have been taught and passed from last pastor without studying the origin or history of a thing, "IT'S A SPIRIT OF ERROR"!! Jesus told us to preach the Gospel, His Word! And we must have Holy Spirit to do that. We have pastors and leaders running around here with no Holy Ghost leading people, and it's dangerous spiritually. As children of God, we need to just stop preaching, teaching, and ministering to people for them to get it right, and to live Holy unto God. We who are doing the talking also need to apply the Word of God to our own lives and live this thing for real. I can only imagine how God is sitting up there on his Throne looking at us down here acting the fool and using his name and what created for good for us and distort it for our own evil and selfish acts. I believe sometimes it is easy teaching the Word, but it is hard to make the Word applicable to our own life. Why is that? Holy Spirit is the one who gives revelation and opens our eyes to see it how God wants us to see it and teach it. IF YOU DO NOT HAVE HOLY SPIRIT SEEK IT AS SOON AS POSSIBLE, YOUR LIFE AND SOUL DEPENDS ON PEOPLE!! My pastor says, ***"Being in the Will of God is not the easiest place, but it's the Safest place."***

Mr. Wrong & The Mask continued...

Well Back to the story of being a new wife. Back to the investigation, after the holidays I couldn't take it anymore, so I called the young lady up and laid everything out for her, but of course she said she didn't know that he was married, and they were on the phone when she clicked over to answer the phone for me. She also explained to me that she was possibly pregnant, and that they were talking about marriage. In my mind, I'm like this dude is crazy. When I got to him and confronted him about everything, he was pleading she was a liar, as most men would do. I wonder why men do that when they are caught. It took everything in me not to hurt him for being deceitful. I presented to him the evidence I had on him, and he still lied. This guy, I tell you. We went to counseling and we stayed together to work thru the infidelity. But of course, I didn't let my guard down. I just stayed silent and kept doing my investigation on him. I turned into my own personal cheaters show. Next, I had to make sure my information on him was concrete. Sorry, I can't reveal my strategies in the book. Honey let me tell you this guy was a busy one. I found out about woman, after woman, after woman, so I finally got fed up and told him I was leaving him, and if things didn't get better, we need to get a divorce. It was me or them. He said he didn't want a divorce and he didn't want me to leave, and I better not leave that house. The next year I finally left. Sometimes I think I shouldn't have left because I really wanted my marriage, but it takes two people to work together for things to work. Things never got better just more woman, and a whole lot more of his secrets. I caught him at different women houses, dates at restaurants, he spoke disrespectfully of me and my children and tried to blame them for the reason he stepped out the marriage. He told those other women that he saved me, lol now that was funny to me. When we met, I had my own everything, a house, a job, school, and two vehicles that I paid for in my yard. He moved in with me and my children. He wanted me to quit school and give up my future dreams. Nice try Devil, Arry Jay don't give up that easy. I was there for him no matter what, but he just betrayed me. It hurt me so bad, the way he did me and my kids. I felt like I was in a Lifetime movie. But it was all good. I remember before all this came about, one morning before he came home from work, the Lord woke and told me your husband is not going to be the same when he gets home. I was like ok Lord I hear you. Most mornings when he got off work, I would always have his breakfast cooked and ready for him, his night cloths laid out, and whatever else he needed done before getting his rest for his next shift. And when he came home my God, he started talking to me and sharing some things with me and something hit my heart and said there it is. Lord have mercy, the Lord was preparing me for that situation, and I didn't even realize it. I also remember a time when God allowed me to see the actually demonic force/demon in him that I was dealing with. When I saw it in his face, I just screamed because I never in my life seen anything like that in an actual person. That thing just laughed at me in this evil laugh, HA, HA, HA, HA! When I say it was crazy, that was crazy! Now I understand why I was sick all the time with severe migraines, nausea and sick to my stomach from around him, that was that strong lust and perversion Spirit in him. I went and laid down in my bed and just prayed to God to help me! I finally left with my kids and moved in with a friend for a while. We were separated now, and it was time to start over Again!

The Painful Divorce

At the beginning of 2016, we were finally divorced. I guess that girl tried to warn me because he did her the same way left her brokenhearted, with bills, and no closure. And he did the same to me. He was so cold hearted and mean, selfish, and a Narcissistic hateful man. He used to tell me that us country girls need of a man like him, because we are desperate and never had nothing. And every man wants to be like him, He is the man. I wanted to roll all over the floor laughing so hard at that foolishness he was saying. But I did burst out laughing though. Negro please, you tried it. Go find you a dummy somewhere that will put up with your mess. I will holla at cha.

Of course, like most men they move over you like a speedbump and on to the next women with no remorse. I asked him when it was all said and done, I said, “Did I really deserve all the things you did to me?” His response was “NO YOU DIDN’T”. I asked then why did he do all those, and he said because something is wrong with me, I need help, and he said he was sorry.

We as women must be careful when we are dating and making sure we’re getting to know and really checking the background on these men, and the crazy thing is the men could simply open to us in so many words and we just don’t listen and pray. Because there were signs, but I let my heart distract me of them. It happens to the best of us. As me and kids started to move on and start over it was hard at first, but I just kept believing in God, he is a Healer. I cried so much during that period, I cried at church, I cried at home, I cried at work, I cried at school, I even saw a therapist. Just to get thru it. For the record it is alright for Christians to see a therapist or psychiatrist, a mental health professional, and need be some low dosage medication. That’s the natural part of it, while God is working on your spiritual parts.

The Restoration

It was around January I was sitting in the house during morning. School was canceled because of the weather, so I was trying to catch up on some school work. I got up to get some coffee and as I was making my coffee and listening to Tamela Mann, I kept feeling this impression on my heart like I needed to go pray. But I tried to push it away as I am getting ready to drink my coffee, now I'm feeling it again, so I'm like what is going on, something feels weird. So, I am like Lord are you trying to tell me something? So, I sip some of my coffee and I am like ok I give up, I am like about to go pray. So, I go in the back room, close and lock the door, continued to let Tamela Mann CD "BEST DAYS" help me get me through one of the toughest times in my life. Especially the song, "HERE I AM". I let it play and got down on my knees and just started worshiping God like I was at the altar at church. When the POWER OF GOD fell on me so hard, at that time I realized God was restoring in me what I allowed that man to strip from me when I opened myself up to him. Let me explain something to you, you do not have to be in the house of God on the altar. You can make an altar anywhere you need to lay before the Lord and pray to him, they did it the Bible all the time. They would go away and make an altar, and pray, then wait to hear from the Lord.

Women don't you know that when we get involved with a man, we get soul-tied with him mentally, emotionally, and then physically. Then as time passes the relationship starts going through ups and downs, and then here it goes. Sometimes, as the women our identity is stripped, our character is tested, our integrity is tampered with, and our children are being dragged with us while we are going through all this drama.

Our good up-bringing is challenged, that man is depositing himself into you, whether its negative or positive. When you have unprotected sex, spirits are being transferred. When you start acting like Billy, Damon, or Tyrone, or she start acting like Tanisha, Bonita, and Tammy and you feeling all weird feeling, transferred accomplished.

So, if I had a chance do it all over, I would have waited to get married and would have had sexually intercourse with a man worthy of my diamonds.

And the only person that can repair and restore all of this is God, and having the Holy Spirit makes it a plus. (I Cor. 6:18-20).

But as I am stretched out before the Lord, he starts repairing and restoring me. As I was in the Spirit, He starts purging me and cleaning me out. Then I saw myself in the spirit and God had opened just the area of my chest and stomach and it was very foggy (the anointing). And I want you all to know God is very creative and he used the alphabet building blocks. He started placing them inside of me and every time he placed one, he spoke it out, "FIRST ONE, LOVE, SECOND ONE, PEACE, THIRD ONE, JOY, AND SO ON. As you know they were the "Fruit of the Spirit". OMG, when I tell yall that was the most miraculous experience I had with God in my Life.

I still get emotional when I tell this testimony, because God loved me so much to come get me out of my pitiful state, disobedient, hard-headed, broken little me, and put me back together again for the Master's use and glory. JEEEESSSSSUUUSSSS!!! (Jer. 18:1-6)

Renounce the Soul Ties & Prayer

The First thing that should be done is repenting for your sins and give your life to Christ as your Lord and Savior.

(Rom. 10:9) (Acts 2:21)

After completing that step, then you would pray.

LORD AS I KNEEL BEFORE YOU AS HUMBLE AS I KNOW HOW, WITH THE POWER OF YOUR NAME WE RENOUNCE ALL COVENANTS, PACTS, PROMISES, CURSES, OATHS I MADE THROUGH ANY ORGANIZATIONS OR GROUPS, AND EVERY OTHER WORK OF DARKNESS TO WHICH I HAVE

BEEN EXPOSED TO OR MADE LIABLE TO MY OWN ACTIONS OR OTHER PEOPLE, IN THE NAME OF JESUS. I BIND AND BREAK, AND CURSE IT AT THE ROOT, AND ANY UNGODLY VOWS I HAVE MADE INTENTIAL OR UNINTENTIAL. FATHER IN THE NAME OF JESUS, I ASK YOU TO LOOSE ME FROM EVERY UNGODLY SOUL-TIE TO A PERSON OR THING, FROM EVERY FORM OF BONDAGE OF MY SOUL & BODY TO SATAN AND HIS WORKS, OF HIS AGENTS EITHER IT BE HUMAN OR DEMONIC FORM. FATHER IN THE NAME OF JESUS I ASK THAT YOU GO TO THESE NAMES _(input the name in prayer here)_ AND DIG AND ROOT UP, CUT, TEAR, DESTROY, AND LOOSE ME FROM THEM, AND DETACH US FROM EACH OTHER IN THE MIGHTY NAME OF JESUS.

LORD MAKE ME WHOLE AGAIN THROUGH YOU AND ONLY YOU, AND EVERY DESERTED PLACE IN MY LIFE, IN THE MIGHTY NAME OF JESUS. I LOOSE HOLY SPIRIT AND THE PEACE OF GOD IN THIS PLACE, I LOOSE ORDER, JOY, STRENGTH, AND POSITIVITY, IN THE JESUS NAME, AMEN. I CHOOSE NOW TO PRESENT MY BODY AS A LIVING SACRIFICE, HOLY AND ACCEPTABLE TO YOU, AND GRANT YOU PERMISSION TO LEAD ME IN YOUR WILL AND YOUR WAY. I AM FREE!!! IN JESUS NAME, AMEN.

Hurricane Matthew

On October 8, 2016, Hurricane Matthew struck our home and flooded us out and we lost everything. and Tone and I were in the house sleep at the time, and it took my sister to come and wake us up. She said something told her to come to the house. At that time, the water was coming up at the back door. I woke my baby up and I cooked us some breakfast because I didn't know when the next time we were going to eat, but all I know is I have to feed my child no matter what.

Afterwards we started throwing everything we could in the car and left. Within the hour my neighbor text me a picture of our home and it was under water. I just cried and asked God what are me and my babies going to do. My dad left me that house for me and my kids to always have somewhere to go. That was the family house. Just like it was when I was growing up.

I just cried and prayed to the Lord. Even in that, the devil was trying some crazy stuff, even used my family to come up against me, no matter how much you been there for them.

But God worked that out to. But as I was going thru that I was praying and confused, but trying to comfort my family, because they have never been through anything like that. They have always had the

"GOOD LIFE" of course I spoiled them. Of course, they didn't understand what to do or how to handle something like this. When the water receded so we can get into my street, and we were able to go back to the house to see what we could save, only a few

clothes and shoes, and a few other items. I knew then we were going to have to start all over again. But what really blew my mind is when I walked into my War Room I had made and there was only one of my prayers taped on the wall during the Flood. This is the prayer.

LORD OPEN UP MY EYES, EARS, MIND, AND HEART TO THE UNDERSTANDING OF YOUR TRUTH, AND WISDOM OF YOUR WORD. OUR LIVES SHOULD BE THE IMAGE OF YOUR TRUTH & HOLINESS; OUR LIFE SHOULD BE PLEASING TO YOU, MY GOD.

I learned that day when we make prayers and petitions to the Lord, He's going to put them to test. And I guess this was my test to truly, truly, learn to depend and trust in him, and to also acquire the things I asked for in that prayer. Because we all know that it all has to work together.

After we began getting temporarily settled at a family member home until FEMA helped us in placement. For about three days I was in shock. On maybe the fourth day after the state gave us the clearance to start using water again, we were able to take showers. The night before I told God I would trust him, even if I don't understand how to, I will learn if he helps me.

That next morning, I got in the shower still praying and talking to God, I'm getting ready to get dressed but I just stop and look up with tears in my eyes and say, "GOD I TRUST YOU" and the next thing I know it felt like something pushed me down onto my knees and I just begin to worship and lay out before the Lord. Let me tell you something ARRY JAY WILL MAKE AN ALTAR ANYWHERE TO GET IN TUNE WITH HER FATHER"!!

As I'm praying, The Lord spoke to me and said I going to work everything out daughter. And when I tell you he did just what he said, people were contacting me that I didn't even know, and blessings were coming from everywhere. When I say when I moved into my next place. I had everything.

TO GOD BE THE GLORY! So, I have learned that God is a Healer, a Way maker, a provider, a deliverer, a restorer plus much more. But I knew He wasn't finished with me yet or showing me THAT HE IS the "I AM, THAT I AM" ....

RELEASING THE OTHER PERSON

This Testimony/experience occurred when I fellowshipped with my cousin's church one Sunday morning after the conflict with my Ex-husband. When I called her afterwards, she heard how upset I was, she told me to come to her church and just give it all to God. When I got there, the preacher was talking about what I was going through in his sermon. I just took it as I was in the right place at the right time, where God wanted me to hear him through the Word.

Women, do you believe some of us were created to be set aside just for the master use? To be completely only married to our spiritual husband?

To be specifically on the mission for God. So, I am encouraging you to seriously seek the Lord for your life purpose and destiny, and His will is for you. Because I have learned that His plan in most cases, is different from ours.

After he finished preaching, they did altar call for anyone the wanted prayer. I felt led to go up and get prayer, so I went up. As I'm getting prayer the preacher starts speaking about things, and then the other preacher starts hugging me, she must have seen the pain in my heart, and they realized something else was going on with me, she looked in my eyes and said oh no mam, "I SEE YOU, AND THERE IS NO

MORE NEED FOR YOU". I knew who she was talking about; she was talking about Clarissa, My Homie, and My Alter-Ego, and she always kept me on point. I'm laughing while I am writing this because Clarissa was "G". She was go-hard, off the chain, rough, tough, down for whatever, adventurous, and just down right crazy! Me and her did so much together. Anyways, the preacher telling me that she had become as a protector for me, because of all the things I went through in my life, but the only protector, I needed was "GOD". She said that Clarissa was connected to me like a vine. But as that day she had to go. I know Holy Spirit and the Pastors were making sure I was getting delivered that day.

As they prayed for me, called out, they started casting out all things connected, and I started throwing up, and I felt myself like I was getting crippled and twisted like a pretzel. But they just kept praying and they stopped and looked into my eyes, (the eyes are windows to your soul), and she said I see you, and you letting her go now! And then I felt something was being snatched from me and I was being ripped, but after some time. Clarissa must have realized that they were not going to stop calling on HOLY SPIRIT and Pleading the BLOOD OF JESUS, I finally got delivered. You do know that you must want to receive deliverance from your situation. My spiritual dad used to always say, "you have to be tired of being sick and tired". No pastor or prophet, etc. can give you deliverance, only God. Can you say freedom! I felt like I had been fighting 10 people, I was so weak, tired, and drained. So, I went home and put myself on a fast that week. I wanted to consecrate myself to God. He dealt with me so powerful in that time; I stayed in my word and remained prayerful. I sense a new beginning in my life. Things we're getting on track with me and my family and we were doing fine. Well of course that old slew-foot himself can't stand Arry Jay anyways. He doesn't understand every time he tries to knock me down, or stop my purpose, he just set it up, so God can come in and be Victorious.

Life Changing Phone Call

On August 21, 2017, was an odd day for the earth, because it was the schedule day for "The Eclipse". Everyone all over the world was in such an uproar about it. They were talking about all over the news and social media, planning eclipse parties and everything.

But I woke up that morning like any other morning, to get ready for work. I prepared my oatmeal and coffee, as usual. But something just didn't feel right. Something just felt strange in the atmosphere. My spirit was very uneasy. On the way to work I made some phone calls to some family members asking them are they ok, they replied yes, they are fine.

But that didn't ease my mind or spirit at all. So, I tried to play some worship music as always on the way to work to get me some worship time in with the Lord. But the I couldn't get that to work for some reason. At that point, I'm thinking, Lord what is going on, my stomach queasy, not really eating my breakfast, my music not acting right. So, I started asking God what's going on? Whatever it is work it out or prepare me for it. So, I went through my day still asking certain ones felt anything or feel what I'm feeling, and they are like no I'm fine.

They are saying maybe it's because of the Eclipse, it's the energy in the Earth or something, and I'm like ok whatever, maybe so. But I still couldn't shake that feeling like something was not right.

Lunch time rolls around and I'm always starving, but that day I still didn't have an appetite. I continued to work through the day, and clocked out at 5pm. Got home, did my usual, showered, to, relax, and started working on the computer. I had it in my mind that if anything was to happen to me, I did not want my children to have anything to worry about when it came to me passing away, so I started my own preparation. I completed everything and was saving it to my USB drive and was powering down my laptop. As I was doing this, my cellphone rang, and it was my sons God-mother, Arry, are you sitting down? I said yes what is wrong? and these words came out of her mouth, “I THINK ONE OF YOUR SONS HAVE BEEN SHOT, I THINK IT MIGHT BE YOUR OLDEST SON, and I started shaking all over and my heart stopped for a second, then she said, I’m going to make one phone call to make sure. She called me right back before I left and proceeded to tell me the shooting is over at North Street Park; I’m going to meet you over there. At that moment, I told her I needed her to be sure because I could not call either of their Dads and tell them this horrific news. So, she called me back, and confirmed that it was my baby boy, my Tone, that was shot.

Lord at that moment, I did not know how to tell his Dad, his brothers and sisters about Tone. But I had to, and we all met at the Park, but it was blocked off at the Ramsey street entrance, by the railroad tracks. A little while after we got there, an ambulance was leaving with no siren or lights, but Lord knows in a million years, I never thought that was because my baby was gone and was passing me and didn’t get a chance to say goodbye for the last time.

Furthermore, to even believe that it was him, or that he was deceased. All the family was there, and we just waited for the Detectives to come back to let us know what was going on. They came up and spoke to us and asked us for a picture of Tone, and I gave them one and he left back down to the crime scene. We could not go because he said it would contaminate the area for evidence. In about 10 minutes he came back with this disappointed look on his face, and said "MS. MANNING, IM SORRY TO TELL YOU, YOUR SON ANTONIO STYLES HAS BEEN IDENTIFIED AS THE VICTIM, AND HE DIDN'T MAKE IT", I JUST FELL TO MY KNEES SCREAMING ASKING GOD WHY, WHY DID HE ALLOW THIS TO HAPPEN TO MY BABY?

My kids, family and friends, we got in a group a just held each other and cried in despair for our Tone. Then we all left the scene and went home, and I was up all night because even after what the Police told me, I still didn't believe them. I was up waiting for him to call me and say "MA, YOU KNOW I HAD TO GET MISSIN, IM GOOD THO, STOP TRIPPIN ARRY J". He would play and call me by my first name to irritate me. But sadly, he never called me. Everything in my life went very silent. I was very angry and broken, confused, disappointed, ready to give up on everything. All these phone calls started coming in, family started showing up, so I guess this really meant that this is a reality, my baby is really gone. The News people even showed up to get an interview. I had nothing to say, but what do you say in that type of situation in this type of devastation.

And the unthinkable happen, I had to decide for my baby funeral service. Instead of getting him ready for the first day of school as I have done every year of his life. Consequently, instead of getting his fresh cut for school, going to the mall for clothes and shoes, and whatever else he loves to do before school starts, we were doing it to lay him to rest. The blessing of it all day before this happened, he begged me to come get him from his aunt house to go to church, he never does that, but that Sunday August 20, 2017, he gave his life to Christ.

Lord have mercy on my soul, Mothers let me tell you that was one of the hardest and horrific things in my life that I ever had to experience! One of my first realities was to go to the funeral home to view his body before for the service. That's the next part of the reality that hits you. It's like somebody standing at the top of your body and grabbing you by the head and ripping your body in half and leaving you there to die. When I saw my baby laying there on that cold table lifeless, not calling my name, not moving, not laughing with that handsome smile of his. I started calling his name so he would get up, but he wouldn't move, I JUST LOST IT, I FLIP IT AND JUST STARTED SCREAMING! My other babies were getting sick and passing out. It was just horrible. It was the worst day for our Family on both sides. That night I was in the shower just crying out to God with more questions because he still hasn't given me any answers from the last questions. Because, I told God I do not see myself coming back from this. This is so hard, and too heavy to handle. I'm going to lose my mind, and just give up on everything. I worked so hard for my baby, to keep him out of trouble and from something like this happening to him. We kept him busy in all types of programs in the surrounding North Carolina. What am I am supposed to do now, God?

In a quiet still voice, I heard God say I was working behind the scenes the whole time. I do things in my own style, my own timing, and in my own unique way. I do things mysteriously and creatively. God said, Antonio was one of my special unique handy works. Even in his passing, I was in the midst. I have my child with me now, you do not have to worry about him anymore. His purpose on Earth was completed.

God said, you will continue to work for your baby, Daughter you have a mission to do. I need you to tell Antonio story, start an organization and you will Name it "God's Style Outreach" and this is Ministry. Make it about gun violence and mental health. Reach out to youth like Antonio and to Mothers who have experience the same tragedy. And of course, his last name was "STYLES". Antonio was created in God's own style. And to mention that day before he was murdered, He re-dedicated his life back to Christ. His memory will live on through you, his Mother.

And on September 5, 2017, God's Style Outreach Non-Profit Organization began in the Memory of Antonio J. Styles. The community ministry began. From Prayer walks, gun Violence Awareness meetings and Youth Mental health information meetings and pushing Life Insurance.

As time passed, The Lord gave me B.R.E.M (Broken Restored Empowered Mothers) which reach out to the mothers that have lost children to gun violence or any type of loss. I have also joined MOMS DEMAND ACTION, I am the Chapter Lead for Fayetteville NC, which is a national organization against gun violence. I was nominated for the "WOMEN IN POWER" award in 2018 and had to go to Washington DC to stand on the panel with other nominees. I did not win, but the experience was amazing, and I met some great women from across the world. I AM STILL A WINNER and A WOMAN WITH POWER!!

It's a spiritual thing; You feel me!

I also joined Epiphany Ministries out of Charlotte, NC, which is an organization that ministers inside of prisons to the troubled youth behind bars. I love those kids, because really all they need is someone real and who genuinely love them.

I have done a lot of traveling experiencing and learning so much in this process, the Lord is doing so much in my life, its mind blowing. I know He is going to have me doing a lot more. But in his timing, it's very important. I can remember this day I was grieving heavy as I did every day since I lost my baby, but this day was harder, and I was trying to clean up my room and ran across this bag that I kept trying to get rid because I did not know who it belonged to. But this bag just kept showing up. So finally, I was like I'm going to see what's in this bag. Lo and behold, when I opened it was all my baby stuff from his last program he was in before he passed away. From the day he started to his last day, what he did and even when he got saved, and his group name was "Authentic Antonio", which he was. Always being himself. He drove you crazy sometimes, but you couldn't help to love him, especially that smile and that deep voice. And just kept reading more letters and cards to him from teachers and organization he joined. I just couldn't stop from all the wonderful things they were saying about my baby. I had to find out who these people are and where they are. I am so glad I did not throw this bag away. Honestly, I don't think it was meant for me to. Sometimes, I think he was making sure I didn't want me to, because it kept appearing out of nowhere all time. So, I Googled the name and located a contact number and called it and a young lady answered the phone and started sharing with her what happened and who my son was. She got excited and started sharing with me that they are in California and they had just had a big ceremony there for the "STARS", that's what they call the kids. My baby was a Star. And they had a memorial service in the memory of my baby. We both just started crying together on the phone as she shared her stories of Antonio. And then referred me to Charlotte because that is where he was located while in the program. After we got off the phone, I called them, and I talked to one of Ladies that oversees the organization, and we had an emotional moment as well after I told her who I was and the other phone call conversation I had with corporate.

She invited me down to Charlotte, so we can meet in person, she offered to pay for everything, so me and my God-mom went that following weekend. They were having an event at the all boy facility and asked me if I would speak to them about gun violence and Antonio life. I met a lot of his friends he made their, the administration and staff there loved him dearly as well. Everyone had their own story and moment with Tone. Epiphany have the most loving, genuine, and sincere people I have ever met in my life. It was so amazing and emotional time. It was such a blessing to us all. After that encounter, that is when I decided to join Epiphany Ministries. I have been going there ever since.

My last testimony I will share with you all, is another time I was having a Tone day as I call it, I was trying to pray, but every time I tried to pray, I just wailed and cried in despair, I was hurting so bad, I just wanted my baby back. And I still didn't understand why my baby had to go. Other mothers still had their sons, but I didn't have mine anymore. Two people came to me to call for prayer. But hands started dialing this person's number. They didn't answer the phone, but a few minutes later she called me back. And I shared with her my issue and she just started praying for me and it was just what I needed. The Lord began to take her into another realm, and she begin to Prophesy to me and tell me what the Lord said. It just blessed me so much because it gave me clarity in my questions to God about my son's death.

Mothers don't you ever let anyone tell you that you can't question God. He is the creator, so if he doesn't have the answer then who does? Correct. Talk to God and seek answers from him about any situation in your life. I was told he will give one of three answers, YES, NO, or WAIT. But I also know he will give you clarity and understanding, if you give it to him.

God used her to give me specific directions and I wrote them down and did exactly what the Lord said. He also used one my childhood sisters that went with me to complete the mission God gave me, and The Lord spoke thru her as well to clarify some more of my questions. When I tell you WOW, I mean WOW? Some of it has manifested, but it's just the beginning, God has so much more to fulfill concerning Antonio J. Styles. (Ps. 33:4; Lam. 3:22-23).

I will have to say that my family and friends and the community for being there for us and was very supportive during this time. His Auntie was taking really good care of me, because I couldn't think, drive, eat, sleep or anything.

On August 26, 2017, the day of the funeral, we were all getting ready, I was trying to wrap my mind around the fact this is really happening, and I was getting ready to bury my child. I pulled my daughter grandmother to the side and told her the Lord put on my heart to pray for the young man that just murdered my son. I knew she understood this feeling and moment because had lost her son, my daughter's father. We went into the closet and connected hands and begin to pray.

I know you are asking yourself the question of how we could do something so crazy. I thought the same thing. But I had to be obedient to what the Lord told me to do, and not try to figure out God's business just do my part. It is all in God's hand now.

By this time the family cars pulled up my stomach tightened up, I was numb, I am standing there with my other children shaking my head, saying to myself

I cannot believe I'm about to see my baby like this. We all proceed to the cars and everyone is quiet all the way to the church. My other babies were so broken as well. We were all blaming ourselves for not being there to protect him or save him from this. I think we were all thinking this was a dream and we were going to wake at any moment, and we will see or hear Tone voice.

We walked in the church and we sat down and I'm just looking around all the people, sadly I blackout through some of the funeral so I didn't remember some of the people. At the end of the service, it was time for the family to walk out to view my baby for the last time. That was the worst experience ever. This was the first day of school, but instead of my baby being at school with the other children, with his fresh haircut, Polo shirt and his denim Levis and fresh pair of Jordans. My Babyboy was lying in a casket. I touched him and I talked to him like he could hear me. Somehow after viewing Tone I wondered off by myself in front of the church, I just remember having a mini tantrum and screaming to the top of my lungs. My sister Vida said I let out a sound that never heard before in her life. I later found out it is called a "Mothers Cry", a wailing sound on a mother who have lost a child release.

Someone came and grabbed me and put me in the family car, and I remember my grandfather coming over and trying to calm me down and started ministering to me. My other children get in the car and we are just holding each other and crying.

Lord knows this was the first time I could not fix the pain. I could not bring their brother back so they can stop hurting. Lord knows it broke my heart to see them hurting and even more that I couldn't fix this.

We now pulled up to the gravesite, it was time to lay my Tone to rest. To see them lower my baby casket into the ground was soul crushing and could possibly send someone into a mental breakdown. Sometime after that I moved out place because my family didn't want me by myself and to be honest, I did not want to be anyways. I couldn't sleep at all. I slept with the lights ever since the day it happened. I remember before I moved out, a few days after the funeral, I was getting ready for church and I heard him calling my name, and my heart just got tight. Another time is we were coming from church and I pulled up to my apartment and the blinds we open like someone was looking out of them. But no one was at home. I said Lord Tone was looking for us. That was so weird.

Reality of the New Life

A few weeks after I moved in with my daughter, I was sitting in my room just staring off into space while sitting there crying. It was too quiet, when tone was around it was never a dull moment Antonio definitely was not quiet little boy. I just kept shaking my head and saying to myself it is too quiet around here. I was getting upset about it too. Then I looked over at the door and it was his favorite coat hanging on it. And it was like my baby hung his coat up and never came back for it. The reality had set in that my Tone was really gone. Let me tell you all something I just lost it after that.

As time passed, I tried to go back to work, but it was too much I couldn't take it. I just cried the whole time. So, I went back on leave until I could get myself together. I finally went to work and start this life with the help of the Lord. I knew I could not stay locked away in the house forever. Furthermore, I had my other children that still needed me. That when I learned what the scripture meant "THE JOY OF THE LORD IS MY STRENGTH" and I have been leaning to that ever since. I have learned so much in this process, it is mind blowing. God is so amazing.

Tone Death Was Not in Vain

One night I was on my knees trying to pray for myself and my family, because this grieving process was harder than I thought. I promise you cannot walk this out alone. Trust me, you will need some real people and praying people around you at all times, praying for your strength and sanity. But I just couldn't do it, every time I tried to pray, I just burst into tears. I was so weak. So, I said Lord I need someone to pray for me and with me. I picked up my phone and I went to two people, I said Lord which one and took me to the one he wanted me to call. Mind you I haven't talk to this woman of God in a while, but I was being obedient. I called her, and she didn't pick up, I understood because it was really late that night. She ended up calling me back, and I told what the Lord said, and she said it was fine, she consulted with her husband what was going on, because Women with husbands, you have to keep the order and respect, even in a situation like mine. With that she could attend to me with his blessing. I explained to her what had happened to my baby and how it was having a hard time. She began to pray, and I felt the power of God through the phone, I just cried and worshipped him. The Woman of God began to Prophesy to me what thus sayeth the Lord. She started to share with me that "**Tone death was not in Vain**" and "**The Blood Shed Was Still**

Crying Out", and "**The Sacrifice Had to Go in The Ground**". Tone I hear you Babyboy. And she continued to share more things with me from the Lord that I had to do. And of course, I was going to be obedient and I did them. The words stuck with me about the blood shed crying out, so I found the scripture in the bible about it in Genesis 4:10. I was like God you are so amazing. I'm with him getting saved the day before played a big part. I didn't realize how many people lives he touched in only those 17 years of his life being on this earth. On the day of the funeral showed me one way because it was so many people there that I knew, that I didn't even know he knew. People from all over came to show their love and support in the memory of my Tone. I pray that it helped young people to also give their life to Christ because we never know when God is going to call us home no matter how young we are.

Let me tell you that Devil just knew that losing my baby was going to take me out of here, I was going to turn away from God because of anger and hurt, then give up on life, or even commit suicide. That would of cause me to go back to what is familiar and die there. Because if I would of went back that is exactly what could of happen. But that didn't work.

The devil and his imps want to stop my purpose and destiny in the Lord. And he is throwing everything he can at me to derail me from that. But what he didn't know is that it pushed me into an even closer relationship with the Lord. Now he is really upset with me now. All he did was cause a fire to be lit in me to serve the Lord diligently. It is so funny to me that all that the Enemy knows about God, but he stills under estimates his power and Authority.

Pain to Purpose

From that point on God has put me on a mission. Sometimes it gets rough, because there is no limit to the grieving process. But the fact the guy who murdered my son is still free on our Fayetteville streets today that makes it a little harder. Nothing has progressed about my son case. I will always continue to fight for him as the Lord leads me.

God continues to manifest himself to me over and over. Even Mary went through losing her child, her son was born to be a sacrifice. She had to see her son crucified on the cross for the world. Can you imagine that? That also gives me a little bit of peace because she is a true example of strength. I guess you say Mary was a "Brem Mom" too. I have learned The Lord on a whole different level.

In 2018, the Lord put in my heart to do a women empowerment conference. First of all, I have never done anything like this before, so I had no clue on how start or plan one. I was talking to the Lord about it, and I said Lord if this is what you want me to do put things in order and give me the ideas, even down to the colors like he did for the Brem Mom name and colors. So, I started with needing a name for the conference. I prayed for the Lord to give it to me. Let me tell you all how smart and creative God is, I was walking in the flea mall one weekend just browsing around, I actually went in there looking for something. But I ran across this real nice store and walked in, I spoke to the lady, and continued looking round. And I heard the Lord say look to your right, and when I did this banner was hanging up with writing on it, and the name of the poem was called "The Broken Chain". I think my heart skipped a beat, I turned to the lady and said this is beautiful, this is it. I explained to her about losing my baby and Brem, and I trying to plan a women empowerment, but I needed a name. She gave me her condolences and conversated a little bit, then I asked her how much does the banner cost, and she for you nothing. I was shocked, I told the lady no mam I had to pay you for it. The Lady refused my money, put it in a bag for me, hugged me and told me to be blessed. I looked to the sky, smiled, and told the Lord thank you and said you are something else. Some months after that I tried to go back and look for the Lady to give her the information about the Empowerment, but she was gone. I was like that was weird, I said to myself, well Lord you must have had her to pass through for my purpose. He has done that before in the past. I am sure God has set some things in place for you all, so He can get His glory. God is just good like that. On October 6, 2018 was the first Brem Mom women empowerment, and it was amazing, the Lord showed up for us and blessed the service. The second one was April 2019 and the Lord showed up again. It just keeps getting better with the grace of God. The Lord had me do the empowerment, so he can show us His power, and that serving him is the best option for our lives. God desires unity among His people, If He be Lifted up, God will do the drawing of men, women, boys and girls…

My Conclusion

I would like for you all to know it blessed me to be able to write this book, and for God to get all the Glory out of it, in sharing my life with you. I saw myself being many things but writing a book and being an author wasn't one of them. Don't be like me and under estimate who God can call you to be. He does not see us like we see ourselves. He sees greatness in us, but you will have to allow Him in your life to get the fullness of the promises of God. That means completely surrender to him and let him be the leader and you be the follower.

Lastly, I understand that it has been a lot of negative and out of order things going on within the Body of Christ as a whole and people that call themselves Christians but are not living up to it, as the old saying goes one bad apple will spoil the bunch. This is my take on, maybe even my advice.

I SAY MAKE THE DECISION TO GIVE YOUR LIFE TO CHRIST AND SHOW THEM HOW LIVING THE RIGHT WAY FOR THE LORD IS AND HOW LIVING A LIFE OF HOLINESS SHOULD BE, WHILE PRAYING FOR THEM THAT GOD WOULD OPEN THEIR EYES AND CONVICTION WILL COME TO THEM TO REPENT AND CHANGE. WE CAN'T CRITICIZE ABOUT

SOMETHING THAT WE ARE NOT WILLING TO BE APART OF THE SOLUTION. WE ALL COULD USE SOME IMPROVEMENTS.

We should be seeking God on everything and waiting to hear an answer. And if you don't hear anything, sit still. For me, when I prayed about something and I haven't heard the Lord response, I have learned to Be Still. So, I would suggest to you don't make any moves without hearing God for direction and guidance. His word says Be still and know that He is God. So that verse all by itself says a lot.

GOD IS WATCHING US. We should constantly ask ourselves is The Lord pleased with us. This is Arry Jay for Real and always. Love you

Made in the USA
Lexington, KY
07 December 2019